Supporting behaviour with science

Classroom behaviour

By Adam Dean

Using the science of behaviour to effectively
manage class behaviour in primary and
secondary schools

Supporting behaviour with science

Classroom behaviour

By Adam Dean

Dedication

This book is dedicated to my partner Kirsty for her support throughout the process of writing this book.

In addition, the book is dedicated to every class teacher out there. Your patience and hard work is inspiring.

Table of Contents

About this book

What is this book?

Hello and welcome to a book about supporting whole class behaviour. First, thank you for purchasing this book. As you have gone to the effort and expense of buying this text you probably already know what it's about. But just for clarity, this is a book about how to support whole class behaviour. But there is a twist, this text is based on scientific truths as solid as gravity or photosynthesis. If you follow the steps in this book properly then it will help you effectively support behaviour. Don't get me wrong I'm not saying it will solve all your problems, but if you follow these steps it will make a significant difference in behaviour in your classroom and teach you how to make adaptations when things aren't working so well. This book has the potential to enable you to increase positive 'learning behaviour' and decrease negative 'disruptive behaviour' across your class.

In addition, this book will also seek to use methods that respect the fact that our pupils have the same internal processes as adults when it comes to supporting behaviour change.

We move forwards with these two words as our focus; science and respect.

Why you need this book

I imagine you know why you need this book. You've done all the things you already know about in terms of supporting behaviour. You've purchased smelly stickers; you've put marbles in a jar for a future trip and you've spent whole weekends building point charts. In my first year of teaching I changed the seating plan daily for about a month. Fact is you've done everything you can, and disruptive behaviour is still happening. Frustrating isn't it?

In this book I'm going to share the scientific truths of behaviour and then I'm going to share with you some systems that actually work in managing a class. I'm going to share with you the things I wish I had known when I first got into teaching. I'm even going to show you how to tweak the techniques and how to check they are effective.

About ABA

Biology is the science of life, physics is the science of the matter of the universe and Phycology studies the science of the mind. ABA or Applied Behaviour Analysis is the 'scientific study of behaviour'.

It has so many applications I could add a whole chapter here on that topic alone. Among them are the origins of performance management and performance based pay, positive behaviour support (PBS), Pictoral Exchange communication systems (PECS) and all of the strategies outlined in this book.

This book uses a behaviour analytic approach to both understanding and supporting classroom behaviour. If you have an interest in learning more about ABA I would strongly suggest you read 'Some current dimensions of applied behavior analysis' by Baer, Wolf and Risley – a fantastic article giving an outline of ABA. Beyond that visit the BACB website and also the UK SBA(UK Society for Behaviour Analysts)

About the author

At this point you're probably wondering who I am to be giving you advice on managing behaviour in your classroom. I don't want to spend ages on me but to reassure you that I have not simply copied and pasted a bunch of stuff off the Internet I will give you a brief overview of my experience in behaviour and education.

My name is Adam Dean and I have worked in special education for 8 years. Before that I worked in mainstream education. I have worked with pupils with a range of additional needs including many pupils who have challenging behaviour as one of their primary areas of need.

For the past 5 years I have worked with pupils with severe learning difficulties and challenging behaviour. I love my job more than it is possible to put into words. Prior to that I also supported the setting up of two autism support hubs in mainstream settings, one primary and one secondary. I have spent several years providing outreach support in primary and secondary schools, during which I provided both direct support and training on subjects such as supporting SEN, autism and behaviour. I have a Masters degree in autism (education) and have completed an accredited course in behaviour analysis in addition to 1500 hours of supervised practice.

I have lived and breathed behaviour in all its wonderful varieties. I have made every mistake you can imagine, and I continue to learn new things every day. Behaviour support is my passion and I am excited to share what I have learned with you.

Structure of this book

In this book I'm going to start by talking you through the basic 'laws' of behaviour. These are scientific laws as indisputable as gravity and with a strong body of scientific evidence to back them up. With this knowledge you will find that you have a hugely increased understanding of the behaviour your pupils exhibit (positive and negative).

After this I will talk briefly through how you can begin to go about discovering the root cause of behaviour. This is only a subject we will touch on briefly as this book is solution focused.

Next we'll get into the nitty gritty of the actual methods you can use to help support classroom (or even school wide) behaviour. Some of these might be methods you have come across before but in this book, I'm going to tell you how to use them effectively and how to adapt them to individual classrooms.

Finally, we will examine how to check in on the effectiveness of your systems and how you can adapt them when you need to.

How to use it

You can pretty much use this book anyway you want. You bought it after all. However, my advice is to read the entire thing from start to finish at least once. Reading through the whole book will give you a much better grounding in the theory of why these techniques work and how you can adapt them.

There is no 'one size fits all' behaviour support technique. All systems (including those in this book) need to be adapted to a specific circumstance and that means having an idea of how they work and how to effectively tweak them.

Stories and tasks

Throughout this book there are practical examples of the application of ideas. I have personal experience linked to these stories but for the sake of privacy all the stories told here are fictitious and any resemblance to real people is entirely coincidental.

Through the book you will often come across a simple task or activity. They are optional but I strongly suggest you give them a go. It will help you apply the things you learn.

Behaviour and special educational needs/ mental health.

This book deals primarily with generalised whole class behaviour and doesn't take account of specific educational needs or mental health difficulties. However, many of the tools in this book can be used to support additional needs provided they are adapted to do so.

I am currently working on a book with a more specific focus on supporting pupils with autism – keep an eye out on my Facebook page. For now, though just remember everyone is different and these technologies should be adapted by the user with that in mind.

Why we should support behaviour

Many adults have a thought process something like this:

> *'Children should follow the rules and work hard because that's what I tell them to do/ because it's the right thing to do'.*

This is not the reality we live in and I'm quite pleased it's not. Pupils and people in general rarely do what they are told simply because they should. They do it because they are receiving or avoiding something. Please don't misunderstand me. Reinforcement does not have to be money, toys or food. I do my job because I love working with the pupils and seeing the progress they make (although a salary is important). In this case my own enjoyment is the thing I 'get'. Often being kind or living well can be its own reward.

You might say that children should engage with learning because it will help them in the long term, and you would be right. The thing is that most pupils are not at a developmental level where they can work for reinforcement that's going to come in 15-20 years' time. Most adults cannot do that. We use behaviour support strategies to teach our pupils the behaviours they need in later life and one of the most effective ways to do this is to introduce smaller and more regular rewards while they are learning.

The scientific laws of behaviour

I n this section we are going to cover some of the fundamental scientific laws of behaviour. It will 100% help you to understand the behaviour of your classroom and thus better support this behaviour.

You will have come across a situation when you're teaching your class something and they say they will never need it, it is worthless. You will have responded with something like 'yes, you will need these, they are foundational skills vital to the development of more practical even essential skills later in life'. Well yes, that's what I'm doing here. So, read on to understand behaviour in a way you have never truly understood it before.

What is behaviour?

So, let's talk about behaviour. What is it? Well you're probably thinking that it's the kind of thing you want to see less of in the classroom. Yes? You're probably thinking of calling out, fiddling, arguing and things like that. Well, yes, these are behaviours. But so are all the positive things you want to see more of. Things like listening, working hard and joining in discussion activities.

The fact is anything a living being does can be considered behaviour. There is an excellent test for if something is behaviour. It's called the dead man's test. It's goes like this. If a dead man can do it, It is not behaviour.

Task: Quick jot down 10 behaviours that you have 'done' in the past ten minutes. Consider if they are really behaviours.

Summary:
- *Behaviour is anything a living being does.*
- *If a dead man can do it then it is not behaviour.*

The behavioural environment

None of us live in a vacuum. We all live in 'the world' and this world constitutes our environment. That environment includes things that do not behave (non-living stuff) and other behavers such as other human beings and animals. This environment (including the behaviour of others) effects how we behave in a number of ways.

Reinforcement and punishment

Reinforcement and punishment are the two primary factors affecting our behaviour. They are also two of the most misunderstood concepts in teaching and behaviour support.

Reinforcement IS NOT something you 'like'.
Punishment IS NOT something you 'dislike'.

Like or dislike might be factors in determining if something is reinforcement or punishment but they do not define reinforcement or punishment as concepts.

Both reinforcement and punishment can be split further into positive and negative.

Here are what those four key terms mean:

	Added ✚	**Taken away** ▬
Increases behaviour ⬆	**Positive reinforcement**	**Negative reinforcement**
Decreases behaviour ⬇	**Positive punishment**	**Negative punishment**

Positive Reinforcement - *is anything that after being added, following a behaviour increases the likelihood of that behaviour happening again in the future.*

Dog sits, you give the dog a treat, dog is more likely to sit in the future.

Negative reinforcement - *is anything that after being taken away following a behaviour increases the likelihood of the behaviour happening again in the future.*

Class moans about a test, you cancel the test, class more likely to moan again in the future.

Positive punishment - *is anything that once added following a behaviour decreases the likelihood of the behaviour happening again in the future.*

A puppy attempts to bite its sibling, mummy dog nips the puppy, puppy less likely to bite sibling in the future.

Negative punishment- *is anything that once taken away following a behaviour will decrease the likelihood of that behaviour happening again in the future.*

Boy hits his sister, mum takes away PlayStation, boy less likely to hit sister again in the future.

So, positive means adding something and negative means taking. Reinforcement will increase behaviour; punishment will decrease it.

Being a reinforcer or punisher is not about the thing itself but about the effect the thing has. If you give someone a sticker for good work and good work goes down in the future is the sticker a punisher or a reinforcer? That's right, a punisher. And if you shout at someone for calling out and they do it more in the future in that case shouting can be considered? Yup, reinforcement.

On the same note if you add or take something away and nothing happens it is neither of the above.

Understanding these basic concepts can be a real revelation and often it will make people immediately start to rethink some of their behaviour management practice. Perhaps you can already think of sometimes you thought you were reinforcing but you were doing the opposite?

Task: Take a moment and right down five things that act on you as a reinforcers for going into work every day. Then on the same piece of paper note down five potential punishers that prevent you from skipping work. Mark a + or a − next to each of them to show if they or positive or negative.

Summary
- *Reinforcement and punishment do not mean good and bad.*
- *Positive means adding something.*
- *Negative means taking something away.*
- *Reinforcement increases behaviour.*
- *Punishment decreases behaviour.*
- *Things that we think are a reinforcer could be a punisher or the other way around.*
- *If something has no effect it is neither a punisher or a reinforcer.*

Availability and Motivation

Let's look at two other important factors that influence behaviour; availability and motivation.

Availability

Means if something (reinforcement or punishment) is available. For example, we are unlikely to ask for a coffee in the middle of a field as coffee is clearly not available. Conversely, we are more likely to ask for coffee in the local cafe when we are talking to the barrister as we know it's available. Availability is often signalled to us in the human world through advertising or written information, but we can also be aware of availability because of previous experience. For example, Mr J always lets Class N go out to break early if they moan. In this case Class N will be aware that going out early is available when Mr J is teaching.

Motivation

This means that we are more likely to behave in a certain way if we are motivated to do so. For example, if you are hungry you are more likely to ask for food, cook food or do anything that is likely to result in food. If a class has a lesson, they find

11

extremely difficult they are more likely to engage in behaviour that avoids that lesson because they are more motivated to do so.

Motivation and availability together -

together these two factors often dictate the likelihood of behaviour occurring in order to gain a reinforcer (or avoid a punisher).

Task: Look around your current environment – what reinforcement is available and for what behaviours? Do any motivating factors apply to you presently?

Summary
- *Availability and motivation can both effect behaviour.*
- *Availability means that a reinforcer (or punisher) is available.*
- *Availability can be signalled by written cues, advertising or by previous experience.*
- *Motivation means that a circumstance makes accessing a reinforcer more motivating (hunger is an example).*
- *Together availability and motivation can dictate how likely an individual is to engage in a behaviour that might access a reinforcer (or avoid a punisher).*

Behavioural history

It is impossible to predict or support behaviour without considering behavioural history. Behavioural history is what has happened before when a behaviour occurred. It could be what reinforcer/ punisher happened after a behaviour happened in the past. It could be who delivered a reinforcer or in what circumstance/environment. So a history of reinforcement, punishment or availability can have significant impact on future behaviours.

Consider yourself for a moment. Think of something you do every day. For example, getting into the car and turning the ignition. Why would you do this? Well it's because in the past when you have turned the ignition the car has started? If you turned the ignition and the car didn't start or if you turned the ignition and someone punched, you in the face would you continue this behaviour?

Let's think about a more complex scenario with a classroom environment. Class 8JG have two different science teachers throughout the year. Mr H for a term and Mrs B for the following term. In Mr H's lessons the class receive praise for good work and are often allowed to go out to break early when they have all completed the work. When Mrs B takes over the class have an established history that good work leads to praise and early breaks.

Mrs B does not follow this schedule she teaches the lessons but does not provide any praise or early breaks. Mrs B has now set a learning history with the class with regards to herself. The class often complain and do less work as the reinforcement is not available in her classes. The following term Mr H and Mrs B teach alternate classes. The Classes learning history means that they will be more likely to do work for Mr H than for Mrs B.

Behavioural history takes time to establish – If something has been happening for a long time and something changes then it will take a while for the new behavioural history to take hold.

So if Mrs B decides to start using Mr H's methods it will take considerable time for her to build the new learning history regarding herself and the availability of reinforcement.

Behavioural history is a vital point to consider. If a history is established it can explain why certain behaviours occur or don't occur.

Task: For a moment consider the learning history you have established with you class. What are the positives and what (if any) are the negatives of that learning history? Is there anything you would like to change?

Summary
- *Learning history is the history an individual has with regards to behaviours, reinforcement, punishment and availability.*
- *Learning history can be specific to certain individuals or settings/circumstances.*
- *Learning history has a significant impact on behaviour.*
- *Learning history can take considerable time to establish.*
- *Establishing a new learning history takes time and effort.*

The flow of behaviour

What makes one behaviour more likely to occur than another? The answer is that behaviour goes wherever the highest level of reinforcement is available (or has historically been available) for the least amount of effort.

Individuals have a choice of which behaviours they can engage in at any moment and they will invariably engage in the behaviour which results in the highest degree of reinforcement available at that time. In behaviour analysis terminology this is referred to as 'Matching law'.

If a dog is placed between two bowls of food and one bowl is larger, they will go toward the bigger bowl. If a human was given the choice of engaging in behaviour A and receiving £100 or behaviour B and receiving £50 they would do behaviour A (assuming both behaviours involve the same amount of effort).

Your class has a choice of which behaviour to engage in during teaching. They could listen carefully and engage in the tasks or they can do the opposite. The choice they make is dependent on the reinforcement available and the effort needed to gain it.

Of course, we need to consider that your class is made up of individuals with different ideas on what constitutes reinforcement, but the idea holds. If most of a group does one behaviour and not another then the behaviour the majority chose is leading to more reinforcement than the behaviour they choose not to engage in. Often the most valuable reinforcement available is peer social reinforcement – this is a point we will consider later.

Summary

- *Individuals will always do the behaviour which gains the most reinforcement for the least effort.*
- *In behaviour analysis this is called matching law.*

Extinction

Extinction is a behavioural scientific phenomenon which you will be likely to see while supporting behaviour change. It was first demonstrated by B.F skinner in an experiment he conducted with pigeons. In his experiment a pigeon was put in an enclosure with a lever.

1. Every time the pigeon hit the lever a food pellet was released.
2. After a while Skinner stopped the lever releasing the food pellets.
3. The pigeon continued to hit the lever.
4. After several failed attempts to get the food pellets the pigeons did not stop hitting the lever but continued to press it faster and more aggressively.
5. Following this the pigeon stopped pressing the lever entirely.

Step 4 in the process above is referred to as an extinction burst. If a behaviour has been consistently reinforced and the reinforcement suddenly stops the behaviour will momentarily increase and will often be accompanied by an 'emotional' reaction.

If for an hour you received £100 every time you your clapped hands and then suddenly you stopped receiving money for clapping your hands how would you respond? The likelihood is you would continue to clap your hands and then when it still did not work you would clap them faster and harder, possibly even throwing a few curse words into the mix before you gave up entirely. This is an extinction burst.

If you discover that you are currently reinforcing a behaviour that you wish to see less of and you suddenly stop reinforcing that behaviour you can expect things to get worse before they stop entirely. But – things will stop.

If pupils in your class constantly call out when you are speaking. If you consistently stop what you are doing to remind them that they shouldn't be calling out. There is a possibility that you stopping the lesson and talking to them is reinforcing the calling out behaviour. If you were to suddenly stop this and simply ignore the calling out your class would get frustrated, wave their arms around and possibly shout 'Sir, Sir' (or Miss) before giving up. But they would give up.

I do not however, recommend you do this. There are always other things you can add to a situation to reduce or even remove an extinction burst and reducing a behaviour should always be an opportunity to teach another. For example, the calling out situation is the perfect opportunity to teach good waiting and hands up skills using reinforcement. Whilst simultaneously ignoring the calling out. But more on that later.

Summary

- *The extinction burst was first demonstrated by B.F Skinner in an experiment with pigeons.*
- *If a behaviour has been consistently reinforced and then the reinforcement stops it will result in an extinction burst before the behaviour stops entirely.*
- *Extinction bursts often involve an increase in the behaviour sometimes accompanied by an emotional reaction.*
- *Extinction (not reinforcing a behaviour that was previously reinforced) can be used to reduce and remove unhelpful behaviour.*

- *Extinction should not be used alone – new 'positive' behaviour should be taught at the same time.*

Contingencies

A contingency in behavioural terms is simply the link between a behaviour and a consequence. For example, a child does good maths work and gets a sticker. The child has now learned that when he does good maths work, he will get a sticker. The more times he experiences this contingency the more it will become established as part of his learning history.

Rule governed behaviour

Rule governed behaviour is behaviour governed by a pre-described set of rules and without the need to directly experience the contingency to follow those rules

"If you put your hand in the fire it will get burned"

Now we have been told this rule and it dictates our behaviour in as much as we are unlikely to put our hands in fire. We did not need to experience this contingency for us to have our behaviour affected by it. We follow this rule because we can be confident that if we put our hand in the fire we will get burned.

"If you run a red light you will get a ticket"

I have never run a red light and I have never received a ticket for running a red light but the contingency is written down for me so I do not need to experience it and I will not run a red light.

If your place of employment said to you "come in and work Saturdays and you will get paid £100" providing you have a good experience of your workplace being consistent you may (depending on your level of motivation towards money as a reinforcer) decide to go into work on a Saturday.

The thing to remember with rule governed behaviour is that the effectiveness of a rule is effected by the reliability and the consistency of the source. For example, in the above scenario if your place of work had consistently not followed through on promises you would be less likely to believe the contingency they describe will really happen. Same goes for the running a red-light rule. If you knew of several people who ran a red light and who didn't receive a ticket might be less likely to follow that rule yourself.

Task: Consider the following scenarios. Jot each one down and next to it write what the contingency is and how likely you might be to follow or have your behaviour dictated by the rule.

- *Your aunty Mavis asks you where you are going on holiday this year you tell her you are going to Paris. Mavis says that Paris is very busy and overly expensive. Mavis went to Paris on her holiday last month. Last year Mavis suggested you go to Prague on holiday. You followed her advice and had an amazing time.*

- *You receive a memo at work saying that checking Facebook on school machines will not be tolerated. Last month your colleague was told off for using Facebook at work but nothing further happened.*

- *You receive a letter from your energy provider saying you have not paid your bill and that they will take you to court if it is not paid in seven days.*

Summary

- *Rule governed behaviour is a spoken or written contingency that can affect behaviour without individuals needing to experience the contingency directly.*
- *The reliability or consistency of the source of the rules will directly effect the ability they have to effect behaviour.*

Common errors of behaviour support

L et's just take a minute to look at some common errors with regards to behaviour support.

Definition of insanity

The definition of insanity is doing the same thing over and over but expecting a different result. I will give you a fictitious example.

One day David (a behaviour support specialist) visits a school on an outreach appointment. While there he is asked to observe a young boy called John. The teacher asks John to do some maths work which should in theory be entirely achievable for John. However, John becomes angry. He flips tables, shouts at the teacher and refuses to do any work. The teacher evacuates the rest of the class to the library. After about ten minutes John completes his work. The teacher keeps him in at playtime for his behaviour.

After this David speaks with the teacher and asks how much of this is typical for John. "It happens nearly every single day" the teacher replies, "Especially if we have maths lessons". "Okay, and what are you doing to address it?" asks David. "Well we keep him in at playtime as a consequence" the teacher answers. "Every day?" asks David. "Yes, most days this term" replies the teacher.

David explains to the teacher that it is very clear that removing playtime as a consequence for John's behaviour is clearly not working as it has been used daily for a considerable period of time and has had no impact. At best this is doing nothing, at worse it could even be making the behaviour more likely to occur.

This is a very common scenario. It is easy to get caught up in the same pattern because you feel you need to do *something* but if you have been doing it and it has not worked you need to do something different.

If something doesn't work, it is at best having zero impact on behaviour or at worse you could even be inadvertently reinforcing the behaviour. It could also be having other negative effects on individuals in your class. Behaviour management systems need to be flexible to the class they are based in.

Summary

- *If you are doing something and it is not working stop doing it and try something different.*

- *Behaviour management systems need to be fine tuned to individual/class circumstances.*

Reinforcement always works (unless it's not reinforcement)

Reinforcement is a scientific concept. *It works by definition.* Reinforcement, as stated earlier is the introduction of something (or the removal or something) after a behaviour that means the behaviour is more likely to happen again in the future.

If you attempt to introduce a reinforcement based system to support behaviour in your class and it doesn't work it doesn't mean that reinforcement does not work for that group of children it means quite simply that the thing you are doing *is not reinforcement*. It could also mean it's not frequent enough or just not enough. But either way – Reinforcement works!

This class is 'just naughty'

Honestly - this one hurts my brain. I truly hope it is not something you would say but it might be something you will hear. With regards to a class or a year group you might even hear; "they are just a naughty/bad/unruly/lazy group". This is an entirely unhelpful way to look at the situation.

Next time you hear or even think something along these lines consider the cycle below:

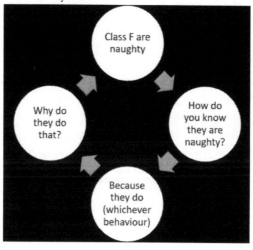

Naughty, lazy, bad – alone they are an entirely unhelpful description of a person or a group of people. They are called 'explanatory fictions' in behaviour analysis.

Translate naughty to - the class are currently receiving more reinforcement for the negative behaviour than they are for the behaviour we want to encourage.

Which then leads us to the question - what reinforcement are they receiving for the behaviour we want to see less of and how can we add reinforcement for the behaviour we want to see more off?

Translate lazy to - the class are not currently receiving adequate reinforcement to complete tasks.

Which leads to the question - How can we provide adequate reinforcement to ensure this class completes tasks.

Summary
- *Terms like naughty and lazy are unhelpful because they cannot lead to effective behaviour support strategies.*
- *Instead of using phrases like these we should relate specific behaviour to circumstances and ask what we can change in those circumstances to support the behaviour better.*

Inconsistency

This is the death toll of behaviour management systems everywhere. If you cannot remember the chapters on behavioural history and rule governed behaviour, I would suggest you pop back and read them quickly.

If someone is inconsistent with any behaviour management technique the technique will not work effectively.

David visits a secondary school that uses a points system in which students can earn vouchers for points. David speaks to the student council. The students say the system is great idea and that the rewards involved are good fair rewards. But the students add that very few of the pupils engage with the system because the points are not given out fairly or consistently by the teachers.

The school has good system with potentially effective reinforcers but because the delivery is inconsistent the system loses its effectiveness.

Be consistent or anything you do will fail.

Summary
- *Any behaviour support system you implement no matter how well thought out will be ineffective if not delivered consistently.*

Punishment and why you should avoid it

There are times when punishment can be useful to support behaviour. Systems like 'time out' can be effectual to an extent but personally I think they should be avoided or at the very least used only in conjunction with other systems. These are some reasons you should avoid punishment of possible.

It doesn't teach a replacement skill - so you stopped the talking while the teacher's talking. But did you teach the listening while the teacher's talking skill? If you used punishment alone, you didn't teach a replacement skill.

It often results in new even less favourable behaviours- You take break time away from your class and they rebel/turn on each other/ learn a way to do the behaviour they were doing without you noticing.

Taking stuff away means it's gone - so you take breaktime away (I use this because it's very common). But now they have lost their breaktime so why should they act any differently. If you allow them to earn it back, they simply learn that they can do what they want as long as they do 'the right thing' after. Best just avoid taking it away or even better support them in earning it.

It creates apathy - first couple of times you do something it might work but after a while children/people adapt and stop caring.

Is it even punishment? - If it doesn't reduce the behaviour it isn't punishment at best it's nothing (other than a waste of time and energy) at worse you could even be inadvertently reinforcing. For example; verbally chastising a class could reinforce some of your pupils if only because you are giving the negative behaviour attention which they might crave.

There are occasions when punishment procedures might be necessary or useful but for the most part it is much better to get a group/individual to earn something with positive behaviour than lose it for negative behaviour. At the very least if you choose to use a punishment system you should have a reward system working alongside it.

Summary
- *Avoid punishment*
- *If you must use punishment also teach a new behaviour using reinforcement*

26

- *It is better for pupils to earn something than take it away*

What's the behaviour for?

Before we start looking at tools for behaviour change, we need to examine how to build a hypothesis around the reason's a behaviour are happens or does not.

What are some reasons for behaviours in the classroom?

All behaviours occur for one of four key reasons, three of these are mediated by the outside environment.

- *To gain attention from another being*
- *To escape or delay something*
- *To gain access to a thing/experience*
- *Sensory – internal.*

Let's break these down into more detail to help us understand them:

To gain attention from another being –
In the classroom this will usually mean either gaining the

attention of the teacher or the attention of peers. A huge amount of classroom behaviour is motivated in some way by attention.

This is not to say the behaviour is deliberately 'attention seeking'. It means simply that attention is reinforcing to the individual or group and that the behaviour has been previously followed by attention. Peer attention in the form of social reinforcement is hugely reinforcing to many pupils.

To escape something – This means what it says on the tin. Behaviours can be motivated by a desire to escape something that is undesirable. For example, doing a task that will be difficult or standing up in front of the class when one is shy. Both tasks might create anxiety and lead to a desire to escape the situation. All kinds of behaviours can have escape as a motivator.

To gain access to a thing/experience – this is slightly less common when you look at behaviour daily and is often more linked to behaviour support systems. An example might be the use of sticker charts where the pupils behave to access stickers, or it could be working towards 'free time' or a trip.

Sensory (internal) – When a behaviour provides sensory reinforcement the reinforcement comes from within the body of the person/pupil. For example, fidgeting may provide reinforcement for the person fidgeting by alleviating boredom or the act of eating will alleviate hunger.

Task: write down ten behaviours that you have done today. Consider and write down next to the behaviours what the primary form of reinforcement was for you doing that behaviour.

Summary
- *All behaviours are motivated by attention, escape, objects/experience or sensory.*

Why is it important to know?

It is important to have a decent idea of why behaviour is happening, especially if it's a behaviour we want to reduce. For example, let's look at a common behaviour such as calling out (obviously this may be different for everyone in a class) why is the behaviour happening?

Here are some possible reasons:

- Attention from the teacher (in the form of chastisement)
- Attention from peers (in the form of social praise or laughter)
- Avoidance of listening to teacher or engaging with the lesson (by delaying the need to engage)

Each of these reasons has the potential for a very different intervention.

ABC Sheets

ABC sheets are an excellent method of recording data and one that you have probably come across before. ABC stands for:

A-Antecedent

B-Behaviour

C-Consequence

ABC's are more commonly used for individual student behaviours but they can be applied to whole classes.

There are two formats for ABC sheets - the first is the long form which looks something like this:

Pupil Name: Class:

Date	Time	Duration	Setting Where and general atmosphere	Antecedent What happened immediately before?	Behaviour What actually happened?	Consequence What happened afterwards	Further notes Any further comments
/ /	:							
/ /	:							
/ /	:							

This form has quite a lot of information in addition to standard ABC. This information can be informative, however.

- **Date** - *This can help you to see links with behaviours and specific days/times of the week such as explicit lessons.*
- **Duration** - *This is more useful for the behaviours of individuals.*
- **Setting** - *This can be very helpful in terms of understand where behaviour happens. If you are in a secondary school, it could help point out a difficulty with a classroom or lesson.*
- **Antecedent** - *What happened immediately before. This could be as simple as 'Teacher asked class to sit'.*
- **Behaviour** - *what happened.*
- **Consequence** - *what happened as a result of the behaviour.*

The other type of ABC form is the *'short form ABC'*. It is considerably less labour intensive and can be just as informative when constructed well. Below is an example:

Date	Time	Setting	Antecedent	Behaviour	Consequence	Notes
/ /	:	Classroom Field Hall Music room	Asked to listen Asked to work Given no instruction	General disruption Calling out Fighting among selves	Adult chastisement Ignoring/ waiting Praise good pupils	
/ /	:	Classroom Field Hall Music room	Asked to listen Asked to work Given no instruction	General disruption Calling out Fighting among selves	Adult chastisement Ignoring/ waiting Praise good pupils	
/ /	:	Classroom Field Hall Music room	Asked to listen Asked to work Given no instruction	General disruption Calling out Fighting among selves	Adult chastisement Ignoring/ waiting Praise good pupils	
/ /	:	Classroom Field Hall Music room	Asked to listen Asked to work Given no instruction	General disruption Calling out Fighting among selves	Adult chastisement Ignoring/ waiting Praise good pupils	
/ /	:	Classroom Field Hall Music room	Asked to listen Asked to work Given no instruction	General disruption Calling out Fighting among selves	Adult chastisement Ignoring/ waiting Praise good pupils	

On this form all the sections are filled in with several options ready to go. All the data collector needs to do is highlight or circle the option that applies to the specific behaviour.

This can be especially useful if you are seeing a behaviour on a very regular basis and you don't want to spend ages filling in forms.

These types of ABC can be made specifically for the circumstances you are working on.

Summary
- *ABC forms are commonly used.*
- *ABC stands for Antecedent, behaviour, consequence.*
- *Antecedent is the thing that happens before hand.*
- *Behaviour is the thing that happens.*
- *Consequence is the thing that happens after.*
- *ABC forms can contain addition information such as location.*
- *There are two types of ABC form, long and short form.*

32

- *Long form ABC has boxes which the data collector fills in*
- *Short form ABC have pre-selected options which can be highlighted or circled.*
- *Short form is less labour intensive but can lack detail.*

How to fill in ABC

It is really important that ABC sheets are filled in correctly if they are to be of use. People often fill them in with a great deal of supposition. For example:

'Antecedent - Sammy was cross he couldn't play with the toys.'

This is not very helpful in helping us understand the motivation for behaviour. What we get is a description of what the observer thinks happened rather than what actually happened.

Far preferable would be

'Antecedent - Sammy was playing with the plane, he asked Tom if he could play with the Lego. Tom said no.'

This is a factual account of what happened.

With regards to behaviour and consequences the same rule applies. We are looking for a factual account of what happened.

For example:

'Antecedent - teacher asked class to sit on the carpet and be ready to listen.
Behaviour - class sat on carpet. Over half the class continued to talk
Consequence - teacher sat and silently waited.'

Summary
- *ABC sheets should not contain supposition or emotion.*
- *ABC should be filled in with the facts of what happened.*

33

Interpreting ABC

Data for the sake of data is largely pointless. It is important to have a way of analysing the data you have collected. The great thing about ABC data is that it is incredibly easy to interpret.

By looking through your ABC you will be able to answer questions such as: Does the behaviour often occur at the same time? In the same lesson? Is there a consistent consequence?

Look at the ABC data below. What might we be able to gather from this brief snapshot?

Date	Time	Antecedent	Behaviour	Consequence
9/9/17	9:30	Children asked to sit down for session 1	Class disruptive, calling out. Took 5 minutes to calm	Ignored
9/9/17	9:45	Mid way through session 1 – asked to watch a video	Class disruptive and calling out	Remind class they need to watch video. Threatened loss of playtime.
10/9/17	9:15	Early morning work	Class disruptive – several arguing with peers	Remind class they should be working
11/9/17	10:00	Given task to complete (maths)	Class unfocussed and calling out.	Told class that if they didn't complete maths they would loose some break time.
12/9/17	9:57	As above	Class disruptive and calling out	Remind class they should be working

There are a couple of things that we can infer from this. The first is that the behaviour seems to happen consistently during the first session of the day. From this we might conclude that the class are unfocused/motivated during that session. They may be trying to escape or delay the work involved. It's also possible they are tired or hungry.

Secondly the behaviour is usually followed by adult chastisement. Could this mean there is an attention element?

Finally, the teacher has threatened the loss of break time on several occasions. Are they consistent with this? Is it having any impact?

From this we can begin to plan some simple changes. Perhaps we need to change how the morning session run or incorporate a new reinforcement system for the morning session specifically. It may be worth trying a new response to the behaviour. Perhaps the teacher could try ignoring the behaviour or sitting silently and waiting.

Task: Choose a behaviour you would like to reduce in your classroom and take ABC data for one week. Analyse the data to see if there are any practical changes you can make.

Summary
- *ABC data is easy to interpret.*
- *Look for patterns in antecedents, times and consequences.*
- *It is possible to make simple changes based on ABC conclusions.*

Scatter charts

Scatter charts are another very simple way to get data on behaviour. A simple scatter chart is included below.

Children not on task					
0-10					
10-20					
20-30					
	Monday	Tuesday	Wednesday	Thursday	Friday
14:30-15:00					
14:00-14:30					
13:30-14:00					
13:00-13:30					
Lunch					
11:30-12:00					
11:00-11:30					
10:30-11:00					
10:00-10:30					
9:30-10:00					
9:00-9:30					

Along one access we have the time of day and along the other we have days of the week. As behaviours occur marks are put in the boxes. These can be simple; for example, a mark denotes a specific behaviour, or they can be more complex involving a key for different types of behaviour or intensities.

The scatter chart above shows children 'not on task'. Of course this is not technically a behaviour because a dead man could be 'not on task' but for the sake of this example we'll live with the discrepancy. The darker the spot on the graph the more children are 'off task'.

Looking at the chart do you notice any helpful patterns?

There is a specific time on four out or five days that most of the pupils are off task. Relating this back to a timetable could provide even more information and could give us a clue as to changes we might make to reduce the behaviour.   I have seen simple scatter data transform classes.

David visits a school to support a class teacher struggling with off task behaviour. The teacher does not have time to take ABC data so David asks her to take data on 'on task' behaviour using a scatter chart which she does for one week.

David and the teacher arrange it so that that at the end of every 30-minute period the teacher will mark down if 25,50,75 or 100% of the class are on task. This is the data collected. What can you infer?

Children on task					
0%-25%					
25%-50%					
50%-75%					
75%-100%					
	Monday	Tuesday	Wednesday	Thursday	Friday
14:30-15:00					
14:00-14:30					
13:30-14:00					
13:00-13:30					
Lunch					
11:30-12:00					
11:00-11:30					
10:30-11:00					
10:00-10:30	Break				
9:30-10:00					
9:00-9:30					

This data clearly shows David that the children in the class are most on task first thing in the morning and after break/lunch times.

The class is a year 6 class in their exam term. They are exhausted from revision lessons and so the times they are most on task are in periods when they are better rested.

David suggests a simple change. For every thirty minutes of learning the class will receive a five minute 'brain break' regardless of behaviour or focus. David explains that although this will mean less learning time throughout the day it is likely that it will increase the amount of on task behaviour and so improve overall learning opportunities. David suggests the teacher take another week of scatter data to be sure the intervention is effective.

Task: Choose a whole class behaviour and take 2-3 days' worth of scatter data. Analyse to see if there are any patterns.

Summary
- *Scatter data simple to collect.*
- *It involves splitting the day into time periods.*
- *The smaller the time period the more accurate the data.*
- *When a behaviour occurs, a mark is put in the box where time and day meet.*
- *Scatter charts can include a key which allows them to show types or intensity of behaviour.*
- *It is simple to visually analyse scatter data to show times when a behaviour is most/least likely to occur.*
- *Interventions can be built effectively around this information.*

What is the plan?

Before you get started on your official journey to support class behaviour change you need to have a think about what you want to happen. You also need to consider your reasons for wanting to make that change.

In this short section we are going to answer three key questions:

- *What change are you hoping for?*
- *Why do you want this change/who will it benefit?*
- *Do you already have facts that will help? / do you need to do some investigating?*

What change are you hoping for?

This is an important question because everything you do afterwards will be effected by it.

Task:

Take a minute to write down what changes you are hoping for. Think about what behaviours you are focusing on with regards to your class. You must have something specific. 'Improve behaviour' is too general. Are you looking to decrease a behaviour that is detrimental to learning or increase one that is beneficial?

Here are some beneficial behaviours you might like to increase:

- *Focussed working (for longer periods of time)*
- *Active listening*
- *Hands up before talking*
- *Time keeping*
- *Organisation*
- *Attention to speakers*
- *Team-work behaviours*
- *Reasonable discussion (after a disagreement)*

Here are some detrimental behaviours that it might be helpful to decrease:

- *Calling out*
- *Talking over others*
- *Lateness*
- *Lack of organisation*

Please note, you should always be trying to increase a beneficial behaviour alongside decreasing a detrimental behaviour.

Why do you want this change? Or Who will it benefit?

Task: Please take a minute to consider how this change will benefit the pupils you are working with and if it warrants the intervention you are planning to put in place. Write down at least three reasons why your behaviour change benefits your pupils.

For example, if you are hoping to reduce calling out behaviour and increase hands up behaviour, why are you doing this? There are several very good reasons that would be helpful to the pupils learning.

Do you already have facts that will help? /do you need to do some investigating?

If you have already been collecting ABC or scatter sheet data, you will hopefully have some idea as to the answers for questions such as:

-When is the behaviour happening?

-Why is the behaviour happening?

-What might be the reinforcer for these behaviours?

If you have some possible answers for these questions, then that's great. It will give your plan some focus.

If not, then seriously consider doing some initial investigating before beginning to look at an intervention.

Task:

Write down what you have learned about the behaviours you are focusing on.

Behaviour support tools

F inally, we are at the part of the book you have all been waiting for; behaviour support tools. In this section I will talk you through several behaviour support tools that you can introduce to your classroom.

Remember there is no 'one size fits all' solution. You should apply these tools in a way which fits the needs of your environment. You should also be ready to change and adapt as and when the need arises.

Towards the end of the book we will talk about how you can make changes to these systems to make them more effective.

Behaviour contracts

Behaviour contracts could be your key tool in managing and supporting class behaviour. They can be incredibly powerful tools or (done wrong) they can be worthless and frustrating.

Many of you have probably already used behaviour contracts in the past. However, you have probably not seen a truly effective behaviour contract like the one we are about to build together.

What is a behaviour contract?

Put simply a behaviour contract is a written document which specifies very clearly the expected behaviours of an individual or group of individuals **and** what the consequences will be when that behaviour occurs/does not occur.

The document should clearly spell out exactly what is expected and what will happen afterwards.

So, a 'standard behaviour contract' from a primary school setting might look something like this.

'Class x behaviour contract
Class x promises to:

1. *Use kind hands*
2. *Do their work*
3. *Listen to the teacher when he/she is talking*
4. *Be kind to our friends*
5. *Use nice words'*

This probably looks familiar. The problem is that although these contracts do set out expectations they are rarely as effective as they could be.

We all have contracts of employment. Imagine for a moment if yours was laid out as below:

Mrs Y's contract with primary school A
Mrs Y promises to:
1. *Come to school everyday*
2. *Teach the children in her class*
3. *Be nice to her colleagues'*

This would give no clear idea of what was expected of you and crucially it doesn't explain what your employers part of the contract is.

Now we will go through the process of writing an effective and robust behaviour contract that will work.

Consultation

Clearly everyone who is affected by the contract should be involved in putting it together.

You will need to fine tune elements after the class has made initial suggestions but if you don't involve them at all you are at risk of:

a) Making them resent and even rebel against the contract.

b) Causing apathy about the contract and lack of engagement.

You should have an initial discussion with your class about the contract including what behaviours should be in there and what consequences will follow.

Behaviours

If it is a generalised 'beginning of the year' type contract, then you can start by just asking your class what they think is important. If this is the case your rules might look similar those outlined above. That's fine, you refine these in a little while.

If on the other hand you are choosing to focus in on something specific, then your discussion might be around a concern you have and how to address it as a team.

This is adaptable to all ages. If you have a class of sixteen-year-old street wise teenagers, then discuss this with them like the young adults they are. If you work with four-year-olds, then make the conversation appropriate to them. Adapt the process to your group the same as you would any other activity. I have been involved with such systems with all kinds of pupil types so I promise it can work.

At this point you should have a list of rules either to do with general classroom behaviour or focussed on a specific area. These behaviours will need to be modified quite a bit further down the line.

Consequences

Let's, look at your part of the contract. A contract is an agreement between two parties not just a list of rules. So, what needs to be decided here is what happens when the behaviours occur or don't occur.

The initial discussion should be with your class and then perfected by you later on.

You need to specify what rewards (or sanctions) will be applied when the pupils meet (or do not meet) their part of the contract.

Some possible ideas for rewards might be:

- *Extra break time.*
- *Free time.*
- *Tokens on a class token board/collection pot which in turn goes toward something larger.*
- *Some time watching a film/listening to a story.*
- *A fun game.*

The reward itself really doesn't matter. The key is that it is effective.

Summary so far

So far, we've gone from a list of behaviours to a list of behaviours with associated rewards.

'Class x will listen when the teacher is talking'

Has become

'Class x will listen when the teacher is talking and Mrs Z will give them an additional 5 minutes of break time'

Already this is much more effective, but we will need to get more specific for this to become an effective contract.

Making the contract specific

The next step in this process is to specify more clearly what is expected from both parties.

To start with we need to take out any ambiguous phrases. For example: 'will be good' is just a clear 'no'. Nobody can even begin to specify what this means without a philosophy degree.

'Use kind hands' is another common phrase that can cause confusion with its generality. What exactly are kind hands? Is this the absence of something specific such as hitting or punching? Or are you just trying to avoid touching at all levels? With such behaviours we need to give a more specific example of what the behaviour does and doesn't mean. So, use 'kind hands' could become:

'We do not touch our friends unless it's a handshake or a high five'.

This is a description of 'kind hands' that even a very young pupil would understand. Hopefully you see where I'm going with this now.

Next we need to specify the timings involved.

For example, as opposed to 'class x will work hard' we need something that looks like:

'Class x will all work quietly for the whole of the lesson'.

Or

'Class x will complete all their work in each lesson for a day'.

At this point you will have list of clearly definable, specific behaviours. This will include exactly what is expected of your class and for how long.

Now you must do the same with your part of the deal. At this point you should specify exactly what you will do/provide when the pupils meet their part of the agreement. So, if you are agreeing that they will gain five minutes extra play time for example you should have a statement that looks something like this:

'Class X agree to do Y behaviours for A amount of time. If Class X do Y then Mrs Z agrees that Class X will be provided with an extra 5 minutes playtime'.

Behaviour contract examples

Below is a simple behaviour contract between a teacher and a year 11 class.

Behaviour contract between Mr F and 11G

11G agree to:
- Complete all work tasks by the end of the lesson period.
- Ask for support if needed.
- Avoid verbally or physically bothering classmates.
- Listen when Mr F is talking
- Keep conversations on the topic of work being completed.

If 11G meet the above standards for 50 minutes of the work session with 3 or less exceptions then Mr F will give them the final 10 minutes of the session for social time in the classroom.

Signed:

This contract outlines the behaviours expected and the amount of time they are expected for. It also provides for the class to 'error' up to three times during the session.

The teacher knows it is unlikely they whole class will stick to this contract in its entirety, so this error proviso leaves a gap for a small amount of leniency and the ability for the teacher to stay consistent while being slightly lenient.

There is also the proviso that the 'social time' will take place 'in the classroom' which eliminates any disagreements on this topic.

Below is another class contract designed for a younger class.

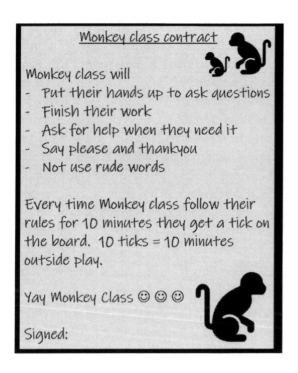

Monkey class contract

Monkey class will
- Put their hands up to ask questions
- Finish their work
- Ask for help when they need it
- Say please and thankyou
- Not use rude words

Every time Monkey class follow their rules for 10 minutes they get a tick on the board. 10 ticks = 10 minutes outside play.

Yay Monkey Class ☺ ☺ ☺

Signed:

Apart from the language being simplified and the addition of a couple of graphics to 'jazz things up' a little this contract does a very similar job.

You might notice this contract also specifies a token economy system which we will look at next. The use of the tokens means that these younger pupils will be receiving more regular reinforcement in the form of ticks which will make the contract more effective.

The impact of a good behaviour contract

Mr Brown is a year five teacher working with a class of thirty-two pupils. The class is unengaged and around 50% of the class are being disruptive on a regular basis. Very little work is getting done daily. The pupils who want to engage with work are getting upset and several parental complaints are made. Mr Brown decides to draw up a class contract:

'Class five agree to the following rules:
- *We will listen nicely to Mr Brown when he is talking.*
- *We will be kind to our friends.*
- *We will try to complete work Mr Brown gives us on time.*
- *We will work hard.*
- *We will put our hands up to ask a question'.*

Mr Brown adds:
'If Class 6 follows this contract for the rest of the term Mr Brown will take them on a trip.'

Thus, including a reward at the end of the contract which the class might be motivated to work towards.

Unfortunately, after a week of working with the contract no real progress has been made.

Mr Brown finds that it is very difficult to enforce this contract. After one day of some of the children not following the rules it seems like he should withdraw the reward because the contract states that they need to follow the contract fully to earn it.

On the other hand, it occurs to him that if he does this the pupils will have nothing to work for. He also realises that if he doesn't follow through with this, he will seem inconsistent.

Mr Brown takes some time the following day to sit down with his class and discuss their behaviour. He explains that he wants to help them to learn and asks for suggestions for behaviours that would help them to learn as well as rewards they would like to work toward. He allows them thirty minutes on the class laptops to research a trip within a given budget and then has the class vote on the trip they would most like to go on. Most of the class are very excited by this idea.

After the class meeting Mr Brown puts together the following contract:

Class 6 agree to the following rules:

- *We will listen to Mr Brown when he is speaking – this means we will look at Mr Brown, we will not fiddle, and we will not speak to each other.*
- *We will only use encouraging statements like 'well done' or 'good work' when we talk about our friends work.*
- *We will not touch our friends unless it is a high five or a handshake.*
- *We will try to complete work Mr Brown gives us on time if we get stuck, we can put our hands up and ask for Mr Brown to help. Mr Brown will work with us when we are stuck.*
- *We will put our hands up to ask a question and we will not call out.*

For every half an hour that we follow these rules Mr Brown will put a marble in the class marble jar. If we collect 50 marbles before 6/7/18 then we will have a trip to the cinema to see the new Incredibles movie. If we collect 60 we can all have popcorn and if we collect 70 we can have pic'n'mix.

If we follow these rules for a whole morning, we get an extra 5 minutes playtime and if we follow them for an afternoon, we can have a 5 minute 'free time' period at the end of the day.

Signed: Year five and Mr Brown'

The new contract allows Mr Brown to look for specific behaviours in his class. When the class is unruly, he reminds them of the contract and how many marbles are already in the jar. The extra five minutes playtime also has considerable impact by giving the class something short term to work for.

Although this is a fictional story it is a story I have seen borne out in real life.

By giving your pupils clear definable boundaries with clear definable goals and rewards you can make a distinct difference in their behaviour.

Punishment systems and behaviour contracts

I have already made it clear how I feel about punishment systems. If you really do feel it is necessary to do this then I suggest that you very clearly outline how these will be used as part of the contract. For example:

'If more than 10 children call out during a teaching session the whole class will lose five minutes of their playtime'

If you do this then ensure you mark down the occasions when a rule was broken so that it can be clearly seen and remind the class that they have agreed to the above.

Consistency is key

I cannot state clearly enough how important consistency is with regards to a behaviour contract. In case you hadn't already noticed, what we are attempting to create here is a form of 'rule governed behaviour'. As we mentioned in that section, rule governed behaviour only works when the rules are followed consistently by the parties outlining the rules.

Therefore, if you promise reward for following a certain set of conditions and those conditions are met you better make sure that the reward is given. This is regardless of other events. If your class follows the rules but a member or a couple of members do something else that is outside of the contract, you cannot take away the promised reward or you are in breach of contract. In this case the contract will lose its validity.

For this reason, it is also important that you only put things in the contract that you know you can follow through with.

If logistics interfere (as they often do) then agree a reasonable alternative. For example, is you cannot provide 5 minutes break time because of a sports event then agree to provide this the following day or during the afternoon.

If at any point you start to question this then take a minute to reflect on how you as an adult might respond to the scenario. We expect to know what we need to do, and we expect to get the rewards promised to us. This is completely reasonable. It is important that we understand that children are just young adults who also have a very strong sense of justice. It is vital we respect this, or we will be unable to support behaviour change.

Summary of Behaviour contracts

- *A behaviour contract is a written document specifying a list of rules and the specified consequences of following those rules.*
- *All parties involved in a contract should be involved at all stages.*
- *If all parties are not involved, they are less likely to engage.*
- *Contracts can focus on general class behaviour or on a specific area of behaviour.*
- *The rules should include specific definable and observable behaviours.*
- *Often time frames need to be specified.*
- *Consequences also need to be very clearly specified.*
- *It can be useful to build in chances to 'error'.*
- *A range of other behaviour support systems including token economies can be built in.*
- *Being consistent with behaviour contracts is vital or they will lose validity..*

Task: If you are not already planning a full scale behaviour contract then choose a specific behaviour and build a 'one term' behaviour contract with your class around this including all the elements discussed in this chapter. It could be something as simple as time keeping, organisation or calling out.

Token economies

The next strategy we will look at is a token economy system. Let's take a minute to look at what a token economy is.

A token economy gives the opportunity to provide an individual or group of individuals with tokens of some kind that can be exchanged for something else at another time.

The form of these tokens does not matter; they could be stickers, marbles, ticks on a chart, pieces of a puzzle or even movement of an icon along a board game style track. The important (no vital) point is that the tokens can be exchanged for something of worth to the individual or group.

I cannot emphasis enough that providing stickers for 'good behaviour' does not constitute a token economy unless the stickers are of some other worth. You may of course work with children who do enjoy stickers for stickers sake, but this is rare and the chances it will last are unlikely.

In the adult world our tokens are money. The money though is only of worth to us because we can exchange it for other things that we want. Consider if you could no longer exchange money for goods and services, would you still collect it just because it is shiny and has pictures of the queen on it? The answer, I feel, is a resounding NO.

The 'economy' part of the token economy is the element that people tend to miss out. The tokens must have a worth and more to the point their worth must be enough that the tokens are reinforcing.

Again, imagine if your money suddenly became 50% less powerful for buying goods and services or if the goods themselves increased in price by 50%. At this point the money becomes less powerful as a reinforcer.

This is a fact that needs to be considered when putting a token economy together. Tokens needs to be exchangeable for something of worth.

- *Summary*
- *Token economy is a system where pupils earn tokens which can be exchanged for other things.*

Token economy 'exchange rate'

We need to consider how much needs to be done to earn a token. If you were asked to carry a 1kg weight 100m for five pounds you might well do it. If you were asked to carry 100Kg for 1Km would you even be tempted? The reward needs to reflect what you are asking.

David is working in a mainstream school to support a child with ADHD. He asks the supporting adult if a token economy is being used. The adult support proudly presents a token chart. She explains that the boy needs to do all his work and sit nicely in a lesson to earn a token. Once he collects five tokens, he will be allowed ten minutes kicking a football around outside at the end of the day. She adds that this has had very little impact and that she doesn't think token systems work for this child.

David suggests several small changes to the system. He now gives a token for every five minutes the pupil is 'on task'. As soon as the pupil gets five tokens he is given ten minutes outside playing football with a friend. This means that tokens are now easier to earn and have more value in terms of exchange.

Unsurprisingly the pupil engages considerably better with the new system. After several weeks of success David is able to increase the number of tokens needed thus increasing how long the pupil is working.

- *Summary*
- *The worth of tokens is determined by:*
- *How much work needs to be done to earn them.*
- *How many tokens are needed for a reward.*
- *How big the reward is.*
- *Getting the economy wrong can make a system ineffectual.*

Class token economies (individual tokens)

The first and probably most widely used version of the token economy is the one linked to individuals. In this token economy individual members of the class can earn tokens for displaying positive behaviours. These tokens can then be exchanged by the pupils for specific rewards. Essentially this is like having 30 separate individual token economy systems.

How to set one up (the practical part)

These are quite simple to set up and there are quite a few creative variations. For example, you could have a giant board game as one of your displays and each of your pupils could have a counter that is either their name or a small photograph of them. They could even design their own counter at the beginning of the year.

You could also have a sticker collecting system. This could be a large display board with names running down the side and stickers being put on as they are earned or they could be collected on individual cards (a bit like a coffee loyalty scheme) which they then bring to you and trade in when they reach a certain number.

There are also online systems. I have seen something called 'class dojo' used very effectively. This is especially clever because the tokens can be seen by parents online.

Personally, I quite like the big board game idea especially for classes of children of age six to ten. However, if you have pupils that can be a little shy or pupils that struggle with behaviour and are thus less likely to respond to these systems it could be worth exploring the card systems.

Being clear

You will notice a theme going through these systems and that theme will be the need for very high levels of clarity and consistency. With any token economy system, you must be very clear about three things.

What can I earn tokens for?

Your pupils need to be told clearly and concisely what they can earn tokens for and then you must be consistent in the delivery of those tokens. Something like a behaviour contract can be very helpful here.

'Class X children can earn 1 token for:
- *Completing work tasks*
- *Listening throughout a lesson*
- *Showing kindness to friends (this means saying nice things like 'Well done')*

Children can earn 2 tokens for:
- *Completing an extension activity*
- *Completing an activity that they initially needed help with.*

By making this clear you tell the pupils in your class exactly what is expected of them.

What are the rewards?

The other thing that needs to be specified is what the rewards are and how much they cost. You should ensure that you have enough rewards to create some variety and ensure there is something in there for all your pupils to enjoy. If not, you will have pupils that are simply not interested in the system.

You could have simple 'playtime' rewards such as '5 minutes chatting with a friend' or physical objects such as toys. I have seen schools who do this as a whole school and where the pupils receive actual vouchers to purchase things online. The 'things' do not matter as long as they are 'things' that work for your class and you know you can keep providing them when they are earned.

It's also important to decide when they can access their rewards. Are you going to let them collect and exchange tokens at any time or is there an exchange day? For example, can they take a five-minute break whenever or will they need to use this on a Friday afternoon? There are clear advantages and disadvantages of each, so you choose based on what is reasonable and achievable on your circumstances.

How many tokens are needed?

You need to be clear how many tokens are needed for individual rewards. This could be a menu style list, or it could be a marker along your boardgame/ sticker collection chart that shows what has been earned at each threshold.

Class G reward menu	
Prizes	Price
5 minutes free time	5 tokens
A prize from the red bucket	10 tokens
Walk the class dog (10 mins)	10 tokens
Visit to R class	15 tokens
15 minutes extra break for the whole class	30 tokens
A prize from the blue bucket	30 tokens
A free pass with a friend from a lesson of your choosing	40 tokens

This this is an especially important point to consider because in choosing how many tokens a reward is worth you are also dictating how hard your pupils need to work for that reward. This will have a huge impact on if your pupils will engage with the system or not. Please do not make them have to earn 100 tokens for 5 minutes of free time at the end of the term. Nobody will engage with a system that is to 'expensive'.

If you are finding that a token system does not work this might well be the point you need to look at.

To take or not to take

Are you aloud to take tokens away? Well I guess it is up to you. Personally, I would prefer you kept this system as positive as possible and only gave tokens rather than take them away. On the other hand, people often like to be able to have a simple consequence for unwanted behaviour and tying this to a token economy can work really well.

If you are going to have a system that essentially 'fines' points you need to be just as clear with what circumstances result in a fine and how much of a fine as you were with the earning element. I would suggest you keep your fines for especially serious behaviours and make the fines heavy otherwise you will be constantly giving and taking points which can be difficult to manage.

Also consider the larger impact of taking points. It is possible that pupils who have points taken often enough will lose interest in the system itself. They may have lost so many points it feels hopeless.

There is also the danger of social reinforcement to take into consideration. For some pupils being chastised and having points removed can result in praise or laughter from peers. It can be dangerously easy to turn a fine system into something that inadvertently reinforces unwanted behaviour.

At the end of the day it is your call – just be specific, be consistent and be fair.

How to give your tokens

I think this is something that you should consider regarding individuals. For some pupils you will want to avoid publicly providing tokens as this could cause them embarrassment and make your reward turn into a punishment from their perspective. For others profuse praise while providing tokens will be gratefully received. If you can you should ask individuals what they would prefer.

Positives and negatives of the individual class token economy.

The individual focused class token economy has a number of positives and negatives

Positives

Individual rewards - The major positive here is that the individuals can choose their rewards which means they are more likely to be engaged.

Competition - for many pupils the element of competition can be a big driving force towards trying to get more points than their peers.

Negatives

Embarrassment – The possible embarrassment felt by individuals who do not get so many tokens is the flip side of the competition positive. This is especially true if you are displaying the tokens publicly.

Logistics – Managing a token system where every member of the class can earn tokens and swap them for prizes is a logistical challenge. You need to ensure you are consistently giving all deserving pupils tokens when they are earned, and you need to provide time for the exchanges to occur.

Summary

- *Individual class token economies mean each pupil can earn their own tokens toward individual rewards.*

- *There are a number of practical set up options including; board game, large sticker chart, small sticker cards and online systems.*

- *It is important to be clear what tokens can be earned for.*

- *It is important to be clear what they can be exchanges for.*

- *You can introduce a 'fine' system but need to be clear on what fines are for an how much fines will be.*

- *Some students do not like to receive tokens publicly.*

Team tokens

In a team token system, tokens are earned by teams within the class group. Rewards are then earned by the team. This is a much easier system to use than the individual token system and has several advantages.

How to set one up (the practical part)

This is straightforward, split your class into teams (we'll look at how in a moment) and pick a way of displaying the tokens/points that have been earned. Again, this could be a board showing the points even something as simple as a tally chart for each team or it could be a board game structure. You can even link it to a theme that's going on in the class at the time.

It's a great idea if you can get your teams to spend some time together designing a team name or a game piece, maybe even a team motto. The more involved you can get them the better.

Choosing your teams

Choosing your teams can be one of the more challenging points here from a logistical point of view. You have two clear options with several advantages and disadvantages.

Table teams – this is the easiest and most common. Simply split the class up by the tables they work on. Assuming your class stays at the same table all day this will mean that the team always has direct contact with each other. It also makes it easier for you to give points to the correct team when you notice someone doing the right thing.

Be careful how your tables are grouped. If you are setting academically and tokens are earned for good work you are in danger of making it unfair for some teams.

Non table teams – this is a good method for fairly distributing individuals into teams. You can make sure each team has pupils with different strengths. It is also easy to split up friendship groups that can distract each other

It is however difficult to keep an eye on who is in what team and often involves you asking people which team they are on.

Who can earn tokens? (team vs pupil)

Can individuals within the team earn tokens for the team or does everyone in the team need to do/ not do something specific to earn a token?

It can be powerful for teams to have the reward of a token dependant on the everyone earning it together. This means that if someone isn't performing the action required then the whole team misses out. It has the potential to create some positive peer pressure and a more focused team linked to the behaviours you are looking for. For example, if you are looking for on task behaviour, members of the team may correct other members of their own team if they are off task.

Individual earned tokens create the opportunity for individual members of each team to earn tokens for the whole team. This creates opportunities for peer praise when individual team members earn tokens which can add a whole new level layer of reinforcement to the system.

Personally, I prefer that the whole team needs to do the expected behaviour for the team to earn a token. In my experience the peer pressure in the team to do the right thing creates a tighter team. Teammates do not want to 'let each other down' and are also more likely to support a team member who is struggling.

The specifics (again)

As with all the techniques outlined in this book, specifying what behaviours are expected and how many tokens will be earned is vital. It is also important to be clear on what the reward can/will be. Will individuals in the team be able to choose their own rewards or will they need to choose a 'team reward'? Will only one team win per day or do the teams collect points and exchange them when they have enough?

I won't go over this point again in detail just make sure everyone is clear on who can earn tokens, what they will earn them for, how many they will earn and what the tokens can be exchanged for.

The positives and negatives of a team token economy

The team focused token economy has a number of positives and negatives:

Positives

Individual rewards – providing you can logistically manage individual rewards it is still possible to do this and thus improve the chances of all class members receiving accurate reinforcement

Competition- The element of competition is still very much present here although now it is focussed on a team.

Team work/peer support – This system has the added bonus that your teams need to work together. This is more likely to lead to peers naturally supporting each other towards a common goal.

Logistics – Logistically this is a much easier system to use than the individual system.

Negatives

Negative Peer Pressure – Unless carefully managed the teamwork/competition elements can become a negative factor. If a member of the team is consistently 'letting the side down' then the rest of the team can become frustrated with that team member and may chastise them.

Individual rewards –If you choose a system where team pick a collective reward this is a compromise. It could mean that members of the team will not get to choose an item/activity which is sufficiently reinforcing to them and become disengaged.

Summary

- *Team tokens is a system whereby the class is split into teams who earn tokens.*

- *The format can be chosen by the class but could be any of the suggested formats in the individual system.*

- *How you split you teams is important – try to ensure there is a fair split of strengths in each team.*

- *It is also important that you have an easy way to identify who is in which team.*

- *It is important to be clear what tokens can be earned and exchanged for.*

- *You should establish if individuals in a team can earn tokens or if they need to be earned by the whole team.*

- *One of the major advantages of the team system is that it can encourage team work and peer mentorship.*

Class tokens

The final variation on a token economy is the class token system. In this instance the entire class earns tokens towards a chosen reward. Usually this reward is a trip out or free time-based activity. There is no reason that a class token system shouldn't work alongside of an individual or team-based system. This is often a good system to run alongside a class behaviour contract because it is something that can be seamlessly worked into the reward element of the contract.

How to set one up (the practical part)

These can be set up much like the other two token economy systems from a practical point of view. I have often seen teachers using a jar with marbles or buttons which need to be filled and this can be a nice visual. It goes without saying that the best way to do this is to involve your class throughout the process.

Who earns tokens

Again, the question of who can earn tokens is important to clarify here. The same advantages and disadvantages are relevant as with team tokens. Personally, I prefer to make the tokens dependent on behaviour expected from the entire class. This could easily be some very key behaviours that you have identified as needing to be worked upon.

Choosing a reward/rewards

Teachers often choose to use a big trip at the end of the term as a reward when using this system. There are a couple of points worth considering if this is the case;

The amount of time before the reward happens – if the class are working towards a trip at the end of the term this can be a very long time to keep meeting the behavioural demands. It is worth considering some interim rewards or even having a scale of mini rewards such as extra playtime or watching a movie before the big reward.

Pupils who behave inappropriately – Personally I believe that if you have decided that the whole class is working toward a prize which is then earned then the entire class should access that reward regardless of individual behaviour (unless safety is in question).

This is not always the most popular choice and at the end of the day it is your decision however when we talk about consistency you can see why I advise that all students get involved.

If you really need to exclude a pupil from a trip that was earned by everyone I suggest you include a strike system at the beginning of the system and explain very clearly what the strikes can be earned for this way you solve the consistency issue.

Where is the trip?

The trip should be specified at the beginning. Ideally give the class a budget and get them to research a few locations before having a vote. If you work in primary school this can be a great vehicle to teach numeracy and democracy. Whatever the case the pupils need to be as engaged with choosing the reward as possible or they will not be interested in working toward it.

The specifics (again)

You may be getting very bored of hearing this, but I need to say it again. Be highly specific about what the class can earn tokens for, how many they can earn, what they can be exchanged for and when. Consistency with a whole class system is incredibly important. If you are seen to be inconsistent by your class, you run the risk of losing all or most of them.

The positives and negatives of a whole class token economy

The whole class token economy has several positives.

Positives

Competition- The element of competition can still be very much present here although it is now more about the teacher vs the class. You can have some fun with this by gently teasing your class that you don't think they can possibly earn enough tokens.

Team work/peer support – This system has the added bonus that your entire class needs to work together. You are likely to see class members encouraging their peers to behave in a way which results in class tokens and even provide support to each other.

Logistics – Logistically this is a much easier system to use than the individual or the teams systems.

Negatives

Negative Peer Pressure – Unless carefully managed the teamwork element of a whole class system can become a negative. If a member of the class is consistently 'letting the side down' then the rest of the class can become frustrated even angry with that team member which can potentially lead to them becoming singled out.

Individual rewards – The major disadvantage of a whole class system is that the likelihood that you can find a reward that every member of the class is sufficiently motivated by is low. You will likely have several pupils who are less motivated and perhaps one or two who actively dislike or resent the chosen reward. This being the case you may need to consider a couple of individual behaviour support strategies.

Summary

- *Class token economy system involves the whole class working for a reward together.*

- *The reward is often a trip or shorter term is can be 'free time'.*

- *The practical structure can be anything from the other two systems or could be a 'marble in a jar' type system.*

- *If you choose a trip it is important to have the class involved with this decision.*

- *Like everything else being specific about tokens and prizes is vital.*

- *Consistency is very important.*

The power of peer social reinforcement

One of the most potent sources of reinforcement in a school environment is peer social reinforcement.

Why social trumps all in a school

When I was in school (high school). I was what people call a class clown. In many ways I was a good student. I enjoyed the work I was given and (if I do say so myself) I was bright enough to be proficient in most of my classes. I had several excellent teachers who produced interesting and engaging lessons.

Despite this I was often very silly. As a result, I was often sent out of lessons. I would then spend the rest of the lesson making silly faces through the window. But why? Looking back on it the answer is clear; I enjoyed the attention I received from my peers. I loved them laughing at me – it was fun and made me feel validated.

The need for social approval from one's peers is a need everyone feels on some level. The need for popularity, to be part of a group in some sense.

This need for social recognition will often trump any reinforcement from adult praise or from the satisfaction of completing a piece of work. In an earlier chapter on the 'flow of behaviour' we learned about a concept known as matching law. We learned that behaviour will gravitate towards the place where the most reinforcement is available.

Peer social reinforcement for young people who are developing their understanding of themselves and their place in society is massively reinforcing. It is highly likely that a lot of the behaviour which effects learning in your classroom is socially motivated.

David visits a mainstream secondary school and is asked to observe two girls in year nine. Both young people have additional needs supported by individual adult supports and reward token systems in place. Despite this they continually behave in a way which was detrimental to their own learning and the learning of others.

The class teacher is very confused and frustrated as are many of the other pupils. David sits and watches for around half an hour and this is what he notices.

Every time the girls behave in a way which was inappropriate, they looked around the room. On most of these occasions their peers are looking directly at them. Some of the peers are laughing and some are clearly annoyed. The girls had the attention of the room. They were receiving considerable peer social attention which was more reinforcing than anything available for exchange with their tokens.

David suggests several simple strategies designed to address this issue. These include the opportunity to exchange tokens for situations in which peer reinforcement is available. In addition, David suggests that every time one of the girls earns five tokens the class applaud them for doing so. These changes take very little time out of lessons but reduce the disruptive behaviour considerably.

Task: Take 10 minutes in a lesson to just watch your class. Observe the complexity of social interactions in the young people you teach and notice how much of what each of the pupils do receives or is motivated in some way by peer social attention.

Summary
- *Peer social reinforcement is some of the most powerful reinforcement available in a school.*
- *Peer social reinforcement will often trump adult praise or work satisfaction.*
- *In matching law or behaviour flow, peer social reinforcement will often be a big factor in attracting behaviour towards actions that are not conducive to work.*

How can you harness this power?

We have established that peer social reinforcement is one of the most powerful forms of reinforcement. Now let's look at how we can harness this amazing power.

Working for peer social reinforcement

This is probably one of the easiest and most effective methods. Simply reward 'on task' behaviour with short bursts of purely 'social time' or even opportunities for members of the class to stand up and get social reinforcement from their peers by performing jokes, songs or stories. Not all children will be into this idea as performers, but most will enjoy watching their peers being silly. In this way your pupils have positive opportunities to gain peer social reinforcement but in exchange for appropriate behaviour.

Pairing social reinforcement with tokens

If you are using an individual token system of some kind you can pair your tokens with peer social reinforcement. For example, when you provide a token to an individual the rest of the class applauds. You could even have a whole class 'well done' phrase of some kind.

When I was travelling in Ghana I observed a teacher with a class of around sixty ten year olds. Every time a pupil answered a question correctly or did something good the teacher would say 'Are they right?' and the class would all point to the pupil and say 'ayekoo' (translated as 'well done') which came out in a wonderfully musical tone.

This is a lovely way to provide peer social reinforcement for positive behaviour and simultaneously provide a better 'team' atmosphere. I loved it! Of course, be careful here of pupils who do not like public recognition or praise as such a system could accidentally become a punishment.

Social reinforcement extinction

One way to address inappropriate behaviour being social reinforced is to put the behaviour on extinction. Extinction means simply cutting off the reinforcement for the behaviour. The problem with this with regards to peer social reinforcement is that you do not have control when peer reinforcement is delivered.

You might consider reinforcing pupils who do not responding to inappropriate behaviour as part of a token economy or class contract. So for example, little Johnny makes a silly noise in Sally's ear. Sally ignores this behaviour and so is rewarded with a token or praise.

Imbedding social reinforcement in a positive way

As an extension to the above system you can even begin to embed positive peer social reinforcement into your class dynamic. For example, you can set up a points or reward system intended to directly reward people for providing praise and social reinforcement to their peers for positive behaviours. Here you are directly teaching your pupils about the benefits of praising and supporting peers.

Summary

- *You can harness the power of peer social reinforcement in a number of ways.*
- *Provide opportunities for pupils to work towards the chance to perform.*
- *Pair tokens or teacher praise with social reinforcement.*
- *Reinforce pupils ignoring 'attention seeking behaviour.*
- *Reinforce pupils for providing peer social reinforcement for positive actions.*

Catch it before it happens systems (timed reinforcement)

When you begin to analyse the behaviours in your class you will hopefully begin to see patterns. For example, you may start to notice that your pupils often become fidgety after a certain amount of time or start to chat more often during certain lessons. You might notice that your class starts to crave your attention more at certain times. ABC and scatter chart data will often make such patterns abundantly clear.

There are any number of reasons these might occur. They might start fidgeting at certain times to relieve the fact that they have been sitting for a long period of time. Which would be a form of internal or sensory reinforcement. They may start chatting because it has been a while since they have had a chance to engage socially.

Task: Go back to your scatter or ABC data and look for patterns. See if you can postulate some reasons for these patterns.

With behaviours like this you can use a very straightforward an effective behaviour support system. Simply provide the reinforcement or activity your pupils are seeking on a timed basis so that the behaviour does not need to occur in order to get the reinforcement.

If you notice that your class often becomes fidgety in lessons, then start to provide brief movement breaks every now and then. If your class often become chatty then give them social chat breaks on a timed basis. This may seem counter intuitive but in fact it can be an extremely productive measure.

Practical implementation

Let's imagine you have completed some ABC data and noticed that your class often becomes fidgety during sessions after lunch. You decide to provide two-minute movement breaks every now and then to alleviate the need to fidget. How do you choose how often the breaks should be?

The most effective method is to work out how often the behaviours that you are seeking to reduce are happening and then plan to provide the reinforcement before it usually happens.

If the fidgeting was to happen every 10 minutes then provide a movement break every 9 minutes. If after a couple of days you have stopped seeing the majority of the fidgeting behaviour then increase to 10 minutes. If you have a couple more days clear of behaviour, then increase to 11 or 12 minutes and so on. If you start seeing the behaviour again you may have made the gaps between reinforcement to long and need to make them shorter.

You may be thinking:

'Hang on, if I give my class a movement break every 8 minutes they'll never get anything done'

If this technique reduced the fidgeting to the point here your teaching was not interrupted by you needing to remind pupils not to fidget would you not be getting more done than previously? And remember that you should be aiming to gradually increase the amount of time between movement breaks so that fewer and fewer are needed.

You might also be thinking:

'I have tried this; my class has a twenty minute movement break twice per day'.

To this my response would be that it's great you are trying movement breaks. Perhaps you need to consider how often and how long these breaks are. They may need to be more regular and in shorter bursts.

Task: Having now looked for patterns in your data have a go at using the 'timed reinforcement' system. Note down if the behaviour happens more or less when the hypothesised reinforcement is being provided on a timed basis.

Summary
- *If there is a clear pattern/reason for a behaviour? You may be able to provide timed reinforcement so that the behaviour is not needed.*
- *It is helpful if you know how often the behaviour is occurring.*
- *Time the reinforcement at slightly shorter intervals than the behaviour is already happening.*

78

The secret student system

The secret student system is a great little addition to your box of tools. In a way it is like many of the token economy systems but with this one the reinforcement is based on the behaviour of one student. A secret student.

The first step is choosing a student. This needs to be random (most of the time) – a jar of lolly sticks, a hat with names in it, really doesn't matter what the system used for picking your random student is. The important thing is that you make a point of letting the class know that you have picked a name and that if the student manages to meet the criteria it will be announced and followed by reinforcement.

The reinforcement can be anything (providing it works). You might link it to a token system or it could be an amount of free time at the end of the day/session. Really it doesn't matter so long as you agree it beforehand.

You also need to be very clear about what behaviour you are hoping to see/not see from the secret student. It can be good to focus in on a specific behaviour for this one.

For example, you might say

'If my secret student completes all their work at the end of the session then the whole class can have ten minutes extra playtime'

Or something along those lines.

At the end of the session/day if the person has met the required standards you can make a big thing of announcing it.

'I am pleased to announce that the secret student today has done an amazing job at completing all of their work. Drum roll please... and can everyone give a big round of applause for JOHN'.

This is followed by clapping and cheering and the class carrying John out on their shoulders for their extra 10 minutes playtime.

If the secret student does not meet the requirements please, do not announce that child's name to the class. You have a choice here. You could soberly announce to the class that sadly the secret student did not meet the required standard and leave it at that.

Or you can take the child in question aside at a time when the rest won't notice and explain to them that they were the secret student. Personally, I prefer option one, it leaves the children wondering if it was them.

The great thing about this system is that it very effectively considers the 'peer social reinforcement' factor. For most pupils the idea of the whole class cheering them on for the extra ten minutes of playtime they earned is very attractive.

I would suggest that the first couple of times you make your 'secret student' a pupil who will almost certainly win for their class. This allows the class to make contact with the contingency, observing the positive results. After a few wins you can make it truly random.

If you choose student who will find it harder to meet the criteria you could secretly let them know that it is them and give them the extra motivation. This kind of takes away from the 'secrecy' element but it can still be quite positive.

I would suggest you save this system for specific sessions or behaviours that are of difficulty rather than overuse it. I would also suggest a brief reminder that the system is in play every 10-15 minutes.

Task: Choose one session this week and run the secret student system. See how it goes.

Summary

- *The secret student system involves picking a random pupil, not telling the class who it was and providing reinforcement if the pupil meets a certain criterion.*
- *As with all the systems it is important to be clear on the terms and be consistent with the delivery.*
- *It is often useful to make the 'secret student' one who you know will do well the first couple of times.*
- *If you randomly select a pupil who may find it difficult to meet the standard, then you could let them know they have been chosen and provide extra encouragement.*

Simple environmental adaptations

We mentioned earlier in this book that behaviour is directly influenced by the environment. In the case of the classroom, the environment's physical makeup can have a considerable impact on behaviour. Look around your room and see if any of these factors could be changed to improve things.

Seating

Seating can be one of the most important elements in managing class behaviour. Where you seat pupils can directly impact their behaviour. Although much of this relates to individual pupils the overall impact of these factors tends to effect a whole class.

Visuals

Seating a child a long way from the front of the class if they struggle with reading, visually interpreting information or even if they are sort sighted could mean that they will be distracted from the task at hand or even not be able to work out what the task is.

Hearing

As with the above this is very much worth considering. This can also be well worth your consideration if you have any pupils who have a specific learning need. Children with autism for example may struggle to filter different incoming sounds.

Equipment

If you seat children to far away from the equipment, they need they are more likely to be distracted on their way to collecting the equipment they need during lessons.

Peers (to close)

Largely common sense, if you have pupils who really enjoy gaining social reinforcement from each other in a disruptive way then don't sit them to close to each other.

Peers (to far)

In direct opposition to the above it is sometimes worth sitting friends near each other to avoid them calling across the room to get the intention of their peers. You can solve this with the 'social chat' breaks we mentioned earlier.

Role models

It's a good idea to seat pupils who struggle with focusing on work near positive role models who can offer support.

Equipment and worksheets

Having equipment out on the tables is a rooky error (one I fell for in my early years of teaching). The 'stuff' is a temptation pure and simple. Same goes for worksheets and books before a lesson begins.

Temperature

If it's too hot or too cold his can affect the way your class behave. You cannot change the temperature, but you can be flexible in ways which help. If it's hot, let them keep water bottle on their desk. If it's cold, be a little flexible on any 'no coats in class' rules the school might have.

Music

I like listening to music when I'm working. I have the radio on at this very moment and the background noise helps me to focus and keeps me from picking up my phone and playing another level of 'Homescapes'.

It might seem counter intuitive but playing some calm music can sometimes help them focus providing you make a clear deal with them beforehand about the terms of the music staying on.

Getting help

The availability of support for your pupils is super important. If they are stuck and unable to access help you are far more likely to see disruptive behaviour. Plan a system which allows them to get your attention without being too disruptive. Personally, my worst nightmare is a trail of pupils following me around for support and hands up are easy to miss.

Giving pupils a visual cue card is perhaps the most effective method. They could have a card for toilet breaks, a card for work finished and a card 'for I need help'. This system massively reduces disruption. It is also a good idea for you to have pupil mentors on each table who can support peers who are struggling.

Adapting lessons

Please don't take this personally but there is a possibility that the lessons you are teaching could be partly to blame for your behavioural woes.

Don't get me wrong, I know it is impossible to make every lesson the all singing all dancing outstanding lesson we would like it to be. That being said, a few simple changes can really effect behaviour in a positive way.

Level of difficulty

We spoke briefly earlier about work vs reward. If you were offered £5 to carry 1kg for 100M you'd probably do it right? What about if you were offered the same to carry 100kg for 1000M? What if we changed it to £500? Now what if you were offered £1000 pounds to carry 1000kg for 5km? You get the point, right? Every time you ask someone to do something there is a balance between the difficulty of the task and the reward being offered.

If the work, you set is too difficult you will see 'escape motivated behaviour'. Escaping the work you have set (negative reinforcement) is more valuable than the reward on offer. This is often something you will see with individuals but on occasion it can be almost class wide.

There may have been occasion where you set a piece of work (usually a test) and the whole class groaned. Perhaps getting them on task for that work was difficult. In this case you are seeing an example of almost pure escape-maintained behaviour. And if you really think about it can you really blame them?

There are several adaptations you can make to address this.

Support

We explored this previously when we looked at how we arrange the classroom itself in the getting help section. Having effective support for a task can make it seem less daunting. If you remember being a newly qualified teacher, you will remember how having a mentor helped make the mountain you had to climb a little less steep.

Support materials

Having support materials that are readily available around the class can be a game changer in making work set seem achievable to your class. Displays with important and regular spellings, times tables, how to guides on common operations, grammar and punctuation guides, lists of adjectives, verbs, etc, phonetical reminders etc. These can make a huge difference.

Differentiation

Good old-fashioned differentiation can make a huge difference. Just try to make sure that the work you set is achievable for each group or individual.

Break the work into smaller portions- Sometimes if you break the work into smaller tasks it can seem more achievable and if they don't finish, they can still feel like they have achieved something. For example:

Maths questions: You could simply provide several smaller sheets/tasks as opposed to one big one.

Write a story: You could break this into several smaller tasks such as; come up with a title, write a first chapter with a character description, write a second paragraph with a description of the setting.

Increase the reward

Setting a piece of work that is extra hard (but still achievable)? Consider adding a little extra incentive.

Create 'levelled' work

I love this and have seen it in several of my colleagues' classes. Rather than split the class into different abilities and provide different tasks they simply provide 5-6 different tasks that the pupils can choose from depending on how challenged they want to be.

Pupils will often choose the work which is easier than they need but then they will achieve this, feel good and be more likely to attempt the next level up.

The work is to easy

Sometimes pupils will engage in escape-maintained behaviour because they find the work to easy and it is boring. The above ideas can be applied just as well to this scenario.

Making the work exciting

When I am working with young children who have challenges when it comes to joint attention, I will often use a concept called 'Attention autism' this is more commonly called bucket time.

The concept involves the presenter sitting at the front of the class with a bucket of highly intriguing and enticing toys.

Children end up sitting and watching this 'show' entranced by the different items. I should point out the system is far more complex than I have outlined here but my point is that sitting and watching these items is a reinforcing activity. The reinforcement is imbedded in the activity and so extrinsic rewards are not needed.

This is the dream lesson. If you can make the lessons, you teach and the work you set reinforcing in of themselves you will rarely need to consider whole class behaviour support systems.

I accept this is impossible with every lesson but the more you can do it the better.

I guarantee you have seen and performed this wonderful 'imbedded reinforcement' yourself on several occasions. At forest schools lesson you might have noticed pupils who are not usually engaged are suddenly focused and enjoy listening. You might have seen the same thing with some children and PE. These are real time examples of imbedded reinforcement.

Enthusiasm

You cannot make every lesson the all singing all dancing performance we would all like to produce 100% of the time. You will burn out!

BUT – you can approach every (or at least 99%) of your lessons with a real enthusiasm and energy.

I have seen this personally a few time. You have a difficult and boring topic to teach. Something like fractions. You didn't enough time to buy birthday cakes to cut into halves and so you will be doing the standard 'draw a line to cut the circle in half' fraction lesson. There is very little chance this will be engaging enough to be 'embedded reinforcement'.

Despite this you are feeling enthusiastic, engaged and full of banter. You perform your dull, run of the mill lesson with passion, tell a few jokes. You enjoy yourself. And suddenly you notice that the class are engaged an learning more than the history lesson last week when you got the class to dissect a pretend mummy in history (true story)

Your enthusiasm can sometimes be the imbedded reinforcement need to engage a class.

Interest focused tasks

If you can find a way to link the work you are asking pupils to complete link to something they are interested in you will have the same opportunity for imbedded reinforcement as the exciting lesson method. There are so many ways to do this:

- *Have the class vote on a topic*
- *Challenge pupils to complete a project on a subject of their choice*
- *In literacy link a specific type of writing to an area of interest*
- *ICT tasks on areas of interest*
- *Get a class interested in a new topic with a 'BANG' type introduction such as a trip or film linked to the idea.*

When the behaviour is linked to additional factors

It is worth noting that individual behaviours can often be linked (in individuals) to specific additional needs such as global delay, autism spectrum condition or mental health difficulties.

This is not a subject this book seeks to address as it's focus is on whole class behaviour.

You do need to take account of individual circumstances within your class. The strategies in this book will work for the majority of your class. If a pupil is still struggling they need something more specific and highly tuned to support their individual behaviour.

Is it working?

In this section I am going to examine the question of if an intervention is working and if not, why not. This could be the most important section of the book. This is where we look at how to fine tune the systems discussed. Here we take common systems and adapt them to fit individual circumstances.

This section is split into three key parts. The first is 'How do you know if it's working'. In this section we examine what you can do to scrutinise the effectiveness of your own ongoing behaviour support interventions. We will also examine the benefits and methods of ongoing data collection.

The second section is a troubleshooting section. Here we will look at all the things you can change about an intervention when it seems to be ineffective. It is likely this is the section you will come back to most often on your behaviour support journey.

Finally, there is a brief look at what steps you can begin to take once you have got your basic behaviour support in hand because this is not the end of the journey.

How do you know if it's working?

How do you know if your behaviour support techniques are effective?

When you know you know

I would get hung drawn and quartered by colleagues in the behaviour analytic field for saying this but sometimes you just know that things are going well.

You have identified a behaviour that you want to decrease and it has just stopped. If this is the case, then – BOOM! Well done you.

On other occasions you may have wanted to increase a behaviour, for example more on task behaviour and you know this has gone up because all the children in your class are completing the tasks you set. Again – Boom! Well done you!

Of course you need to keep a close eye on this and make changes if you see things going down-hill. If things are working well though, the last things I would want to do is give you more work that you don't need to do.

But sometimes you don't (additional data)

Quite often you won't know for sure. The reduction or increase in behaviour will be gradual and not obvious enough for you to point at it and just go 'Yup – all better now'. This being the case additional data can be your friend.

Continued ABC and scatter graphs-

The easiest way to see if your interventions are working or not is to keep going with the ABC data or scatter graphs that you were doing before your interventions. Quite simply if you keep going with the ABC data and you notice a reduction in the behaviour you are looking to reduce you can feel happy that your intervention is working! The same goes for Scatter charts.

For example, look at the two scatter charts below. One is taken before a behaviour contract and one several weeks after. It shows a clear increase in on task behaviour:

Children on task					
0%-25%					
25%-50%					
50%-75%					
75%-100%					
	Monday	Tuesday	Wednesday	Thursday	Friday
14:30-15:00					
14:00-14:30					
13:30-14:00					
13:00-13:30					
Lunch					
11:30-12:00					
11:00-11:30					
10:30-11:00					
10:00-10:30	Break				
9:30-10:00					
9:00-9:30					

Children on task with behaviour contract					
0%-25%					
25%-50%					
50%-75%					
75%-100%					
	Monday	Tuesday	Wednesday	Thursday	Friday
14:30-15:00					
14:00-14:30					
13:30-14:00					
13:00-13:30					
Lunch					
11:30-12:00					
11:00-11:30					
10:30-11:00					
10:00-10:30	Break				
9:30-10:00					
9:00-9:30					

As well as showing you that what you are doing is working this can also be excellent progress data to show outside visitors.

Frequency

To get an idea of the frequency of a behaviour simply take a tally of how often the behaviour happens over a period of time and then divide the frequency by the minutes or hours the behaviour was observed for. This will give you a 'times per minute' (or rate) number. This number be useful if you really need to dig down into a behaviour to see if it really is increasing or decreasing. It's great for graphing, if you like graphing that is.

Duration

Simply add up the amount of time a behaviour is displayed during a given time to give you a total duration. This can also be helpful for really digging down into specific behaviours. For example, 'on task behaviour' for a class. Again, great for graphing.

Permanent products

This is a great one for measuring the impact of your intervention on how much work is being done. You can simply measure the amount of work completed in specific sessions. For example; number of words written per pupil or number of maths questions completed.

PLAYCHECK

PLACHECK is short for 'Planned Activity Check' and could be the easiest and least labour-intensive method to take data on a whole class. Simply choose a time period (the smaller the better) let's say ten minutes. You set a timer for ten minutes and at the end of every ten minutes you look up and record how many children are engaged in the activity that they should be working on.

Let's say you are trying to improve 'on task' behaviour. In this case you would set your timer for ten minutes and at the end of the ten minutes you would look up and count how many children are engaged in the work set. You jot this number down and then reset the timer again.

Repeat.

The morale boosting advantage of graphing

Okay – you don't have to graph anything. But honestly graphing can be a wonderful little morale booster for you especially if you are dealing with behaviour in a challenging class and seeing very little direct impact.

Lets say you are working on swearing in class behaviour with a group of year nines. You really don't feel like you are making a difference. It starts to feel like an insurmountable task. You decide to take some frequency data and it looks like this.

Day	Swear words per hour
1	20
2	23
3	26
4	19
5	12
6	15
7	14
8	16
9	11
10	10
11	9
12	13
13	11
14	7
15	7
16	8

You decide to put it into a line graph with a trend line – the graph looks like this.

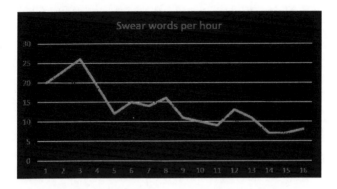

Now you insert a forecast line which looks like this.

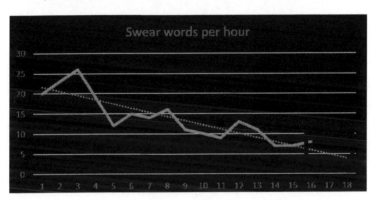

At this point you have clear visual evidence that what you are doing is highly effective in reducing the behaviour. You also have a clear predication that given another few days or weeks you will have the behaviour fully under control.

Take a snapshot

You may decide you do not need to take ongoing data on behaviours because they are clearly at a low (or high level). This being the case I would advise that you still take occasional 'snapshot' data on a behaviour just to check things are still working.

If a system becomes less effective over time you will not notice until it is very clear. If you take the odd snapshot it will flag up the need for you to examine and adapt your support strategies before they become truly ineffective.

Summary

- *Sometimes you will know your behaviour support systems are working simply because things have clearly changed.*

- *Sometimes you will need clearer data to show if it is working or not.*

- *You can continue to take ABC or Scatter data and compare the data before and after the intervention.*

- *You can take data on frequency or duration.*

- *You can use the PLACHECK system.*

- *You can record a 'permanent product' such as work completed.*

- *It can be useful to graph data for a visual representation of how effective a system is.*

- *If you do not take ongoing data it can be worth taking occasional 'snap shot' data just to check things are working.*

Why it's not working and what you can change!

There are several reasons why you might be having difficulties getting your behaviour support strategies to work effectively. Below are a few of them and how you can change things up for better results.

It's not reinforcement

Pure and simple the thing you are using is simply not reinforcement. It might be a 'nice thing' but it's not reinforcement. Even if your class chose it, that doesn't mean its reinforcement. Remember: reinforcement always works. That's a scientific fact.

If you suspect your intervention is not working because the 'reward' is not a reinforcer then you should test out other reinforcers with your class. Perhaps it would be worth discussing this with your class or your staff team to see if you can work out the problem.

It's not regular enough

It is possible that the reinforcement itself is just fine. It's just not being delivered often enough. Imagine if you got paid once per year. Same amount, just only once a year. Somehow the idea isn't very appealing is it.

Try offering the reinforcement on a more regular basis but in smaller chunks. For example, instead of working all day for ten minutes free time suggest to your class that they stay focuses for one hour and get two minutes free time.

The other alternative is to turn your system into a token economy. They need to work all day for the reward but they earn a token every 10 minutes. This can often make all the difference.

You're not providing enough of it

The reinforcement is great but you're not offering enough of it. How much could you have your salary lowered by before you gave up your job? Money is a highly effective reinforcer because you can exchange it for almost any other reinforcer (including food and warmth) but depending on individual and social political circumstances we expect a certain amount of this magic reinforcer to do a certain job. In many ways this is no different for our pupils.

Maybe thirty seconds 'social time' just isn't enough. But maybe one minute would be.

Contacting reinforcement (contingencies)

In the behavioural science section, we discussed contingencies. If your class never get a chance to make contact with the contingency or gain access to the reinforcers on offer. This being the case, they will not learn that the behaviour you are requesting is really going to result in the reinforcement on offer or how it feels to receive that reinforcement.

Often the answer to this is to start easy so that they contact the contingency and then gradually make it more difficult. For example, if you are looking for 'on task' behaviour. You might start by setting the target only a tiny bit above what the class are already achieving.

If they are on task for 40% of a session currently. You might set the target at 45% so that the class can access the reinforcer. Then set it at 55%, 60% and so on until you get nearer the 90%-95% mark.

It's working for the 95%

You may implement a fantastic behaviour support system that works for 95% of your class but not for the final 5% (1-2 pupils). This is completely normal and you should try not to let it affect the rest of your class benefiting from the system you've put in place.

It just means that you have some pupils who would benefit from individualised behaviour support. This is something that you can do without effecting the prime support system.

Other stuff is more reinforcing

Sorry but sometimes other stuff is more reinforcing than what you have on offer. Fiddling and chatting and joking around all come with a huge amount of peer social reinforcement. For your system to work your systems need to contend with what they get from those factors. In this case you need to consider all the factors discussed so far in this chapter.

You may also consider factoring in the 'other stuff' into your strategy. For example, building in social peer reinforcement as we discussed in the chapter on that topic.

The balance

Essentially any behaviour support system is about getting an effective balance between what you are asking your pupils to do vs the reinforcement available including the frequency, quantity and quality of the reinforcement itself.

Summary

- *Are you sure what you are offering is reinforcement?*
- *If not, you can discuss this with your class and try new things.*
- *The reinforcement might need to be delivered more often to be effective.*
- *You might need to provide a larger amount of reinforcement for it to be effective.*
- *Have the class contacted the reinforcement? If not you need to arrange things so that they can or the system will not be effective.*
- *A system will sometimes work for most but not all the class.*
- *In these circumstances individual behaviour support strategies may be required.*
- *Sometimes extraneous factors are more reinforcing that the rewards you are offering.*
- *If this is the case, you need to consider all of the above.*
- *You could also consider finding a way to work those extraneous factors into your system.*

- *Essentially the key is finding a balance between the amount and difficulty of the task vs the quality, quantity and frequency of the reinforcement.*

It's working – that's great but what now? – teaching self-management

S o – you put an intervention in place, and you have successfully reduced or increased whatever your focus behaviour was. Now you can sit back and relax with a glass of wine, a Snickers Ice Cream and an episode of your favourite sitcom. Or can you?

Well, yes you can. For a little while at least and then you can crack on with your marking and planning. But after that come back to this question of behaviour support for a little while.

You see, most of the behaviours you will be seeking to address with your whole class system are behaviours that are actually vital to the real world after pupils exit the education system. Behaviours such as being on task, social skills, politely asking questions as opposed to calling out are all vital to real life. And (unfortunately) we are not reinforced with additional time off, trips or time on the I-pad for engaging in these behaviours when we are adults.

Your job now is to help your pupils learn to 'self-manage' these behaviours so that they can reach their full potential as productive members of humanity and live happy fulfilled lives.

We need to get to a place where the reinforcement available for being on task is intrinsic (coming from within) as opposed to extrinsic (coming from someone or something else). You for example have read this entire book on behaviour management. Did someone give you a token or a token for every chapter? I would assume not.

The reinforcement came from you. You may have congratulated yourself or you may have been motivated by the fact that at the end of the book you would be better able to manage class behaviour. You may have even forced yourself through the text one word at a time in the painful knowledge that the more you read the closer to the end you were. I hope not but you see the point.

How do we teach our pupils to self-manage behaviours such as on task behaviour, listening to others, social etiquette or resisting the PlayStation to get more work done?

Gradually fade systems out

The only way children can contact this kind of intrinsic reinforcement is if we help them to do so. The trick is to slowly and methodically 'fade' the systems you are using until they are no longer needed.

For example, let's say you start with a system that requires 10 minutes of a behaviour to gain a token. You run with this for a couple of weeks until it is consistently achieved. Then you increase the amount of time to 11, 15, or possibly even 20 minutes.

If during this your system stops working, you have changed the parameters too quickly. The idea is to very gradually reduce your extrinsic rewards or the work expected to achieve the same awards until the awards are no longer needed.

Your pupils might not be ready for the total removal of these systems and that's okay. We are looking to support at a pace that is helpful to them. But if you can teach your pupils to be even a little more self-sufficient you have done a great thing.

Self-management techniques

You can directly teach some self-management strategies depending on the level of understanding your pupils possess. Below are a couple of ideas.

Breaking tasks down

Teaching pupils to break down tasks themselves into smaller tasks is a great skill for self -management, especially for on task behaviour.

Self-managed breaks and rewards

Personally, when I am working on a book or some other kind of work, I find it useful to take a short break every now and then. For example, during the writing of this book in my summer break I stopped once every two hours to watch an episode of 'The office'. This helped keep me on task.

General self-management

Everyone has their own tricks that help them self-manage their own behaviour. Some need to fidget to stay focussed, some need music, some of us need to get up and walk around occasionally. If you can teach your pupils to access their own techniques in a way which is helpful and not disruptive you will have done them a huge favour.

Thank you and a plea

That's it – we are all done (at least for now) I truly hope that this book has been of help to you. I hope it will be a tool you can use in supporting positive behaviour in your pupils and I hope it continues to be helpful in the future.

I want to take a moment to thank you for buying my book. It was truly a labour of love to share all the things I have learned about behaviour support with you, my colleagues from around the world. It gives me great pleasure to imagine you applying what you have learned in this book to your class.

The favour

I have a favour to ask (well actually two). If you have found this book helpful in any way. If it has lightened your load. Then please, please consider **posting a review on Amazon**. I cannot emphasise how important reviews are to get this book out to more teachers worldwide. It only takes a second and would make so much difference.

In addition – if you have enjoyed this book and found it useful please share it with your friends and colleagues. Thank you.

Try my other books

At present this is my first and only book. However, I am working on more books as we speak so join the face book group for updates on my forthcoming titles which will address behaviour support for pupils with autism and behaviour support for individual pupils in the classroom.